IMAGES
of America

CHATHAM

Margaret C. (Peg) Keisler, born in Chatham in 1911, has resided on Fairmount Avenue all her life (except for a brief period while earning a degree in zoology at Wellesley College). She is beyond question the borough's greatest historical treasure. Her knowledge of her home town is encyclopedic, her ability to marshal facts is impressive, and her willingness to share her comprehensive information and illustrative materials is gracious and genuine. I would never have undertaken the project unless Peg endorsed it. That seal of approval meant that her vast knowledge would be mine—on loan.

John T. Cunningham

IMAGES
of America

CHATHAM

John T. Cunningham

ARCADIA

First published 1997
Copyright © John T. Cunningham, 1997

ISBN 0-7524-0830-5

Published by Arcadia Publishing,
an imprint of the Chalford Publishing Corporation,
One Washington Center, Dover, New Hampshire 03820.
Printed in Great Britain

Library of Congress Cataloging-in-Publication Data applied for

In this 1940 setting in her Chatham home, Betty Jane Ross heard tales of the borough's olden days from her Grandmother Webster. Betty's father, noted photographer Richmond H. Ross, who settled in Chatham in 1936, snapped the scene. Many other Ross photos appear in this book.

Contents

Acknowledgments

Lester Lehman, president of the Chatham Historical Society, and a small committee assembled by him in February of 1997 expressed enthusiastic support for this photographic history. He and the committee saw it as a logical extension of the Society's fine official history, *Chatham: At the Crossing of the Fishawack*, published in 1967. A week after the first session, several members of the Society committee began sifting through the organization's impressive picture files, providing far more material than I possibly could use. My long-time research assistant, Howard W. Wiseman, whom I consider to be New Jersey's best picture historian, led the way. That vital corps of researchers is pictured below, from left to right: Kay Archer, Andy Bobeck (see below), John Archer, Les Lehman, Peg Keisler, Jan Westfall, and Howard Wiseman. Others, not pictured, who helped were Diane O'Brien, director, and her assistants at the Library of the Chathams. We thank as well Mayor Barbara Hall and the staff in Chatham Borough Hall.

Andy (known professionally as Andrew H. Bobeck) stopped by early in the picture search to lend a few photos from his collection. He stayed to inspect carefully every photo in this book and then used his computer to revitalize or restore any that were dim, spotted, cracked, or otherwise imperfect. More than 150 such photos were improved by Andy. Chatham, the committee, and I owe him a heartfelt vote of thanks.

John T. Cunningham

Introduction

Chatham Borough cannot boast of a county courthouse square, a tree-shaded university campus, or a bloody hill where an esteemed general fell in battle. It is not a haven for Nobel Prize winners, best-selling novelists, or revered Olympian heroes or heroines. It needs none of these.

Chatham is Main Street, where life always has been reasonably predictable, where history is vital, and where good shops survive despite the pressures of nearby giant malls. Main Street is a mere 1.5 miles long, from the high tension wires on the west to the wide Passaic River on the east, and the entire town is less than 2.8 square miles in area.

The placid Passaic, scarcely noticed today by residents or those passing swiftly along Main Street, was vital in the nineteenth and early twentieth centuries for both mill owners and summer vacationers who found sports and recreation on the stream. The successive bridges across the Passaic were landmarks. Today the crossing is obscured beneath the huge overpasses and traffic circles that carry State Route 24 around the borough rather than through it.

The first bridge was built about 1730 by John Day, an Essex County farmer-merchant who had come five years earlier to acquire a plantation that fronted on each side of the river for about 4,000 feet. Day's span was low-level, scarcely above the surface, and easily flooded when heavy spring or fall rains turned the normally lamb-like stream into a roaring ogre.

Lenape Indians bestowed the name Passaic, although exactly how they might have spelled it will never be known, as those first inhabitants had no written language. At least fifty variations on the name are known, all of them the fancies of settlers who wrote what they thought the first inhabitants had said or meant. Fishawack was one of the variations. Chatham tradition (and the official history) accepts this as the preferred name.

The fledgling village naturally became "Day's Bridge." Settlers drifted in from Newark or New England, nearly all farmers and fervent Presbyterians, although the influx was not heavy. As the American Revolution neared, only about twenty-five buildings stood along the principal street, and the place really had no lasting name.

In 1773, however, the settlement gained an enduring name. Advertisements in the *New York Gazette* directed that all letters and other communications henceforth must be addressed to "Chatham on the Passaick River" ("Passaick" was a common spelling). The name Chatham honored William Pitt, the English Earl of Chatham and a celebrated champion of colonial America's civil liberties.

In 1806, completion of the toll-financed Morris Turnpike accelerated development slightly. Pikes (toll stations) made this New Jersey's first toll road. It coincided with Main Street on its way west through town. Many toll-haters swerved southward to ride the "shunpike." The road bears that name to this day.

If only one day could be chosen as most vital in Chatham's history, it would be September 14, 1837, when the first train on the new Morris & Essex Railroad crossed a high stone arch bridge over the river and stopped in town. The train linked Chatham with Newark and New York City. Commuting to work in Newark and New York soon became a Chatham way-of-life. Commuters dominated Chatham's political, economic, and social life until well after

World War II.

After the Civil War, the railroad also brought summer visitors to enjoy what they considered splendidly cool breezes and simple vacation pleasures. Large resort hotels flourished as the nineteenth century evolved into the twentieth. But automobiles and trains to the Jersey Shore or the Adirondack Mountains lured those vacationers to more distant attractions by the end of World War I.

As the town evolved slowly through the decades, many residents rightfully asked, "Where, exactly, is Chatham?" Its early houses and business establishments were on both sides of the river. In 1790, residents on the south side of Main Street lived in Morris Township. Those on the north side of Main resided in Hanover Township. The confusion, particularly in regards to tax payments, was horrendous.

That confusion lessened in 1798, when Chatham Township was formed, with a sprawling area that included several other villages that are also now independent towns. The central village called Chatham withdrew from Chatham Township in 1897 and became Chatham Borough. Free at last, the borough in essence had gained its liberty by seceding from itself.

When steam and electricity replaced waterpower, mill owners either could not or would not keep up with such innovations. The old mills disappeared one by one. The borough's major industry then became the growing of roses in huge greenhouses in several parts of the borough. By 1910, eleven rose growers operated about seventy greenhouses in the borough. All evidence of the rose industry has vanished.

For the most part, however, few places are as lasting as Chatham, where change is a matter of degree rather than kind. Several Main Street buildings date to the eighteenth century. The business area has been declared a historic district.

The past is always present. Chathamites often celebrate themselves and their past, in ceremonies, pageants, parades, traditions, and reunions. Townspeople love the sounds of bands; and marching feet have resounded on Main Street since Revolutionary War days, when fifes and drums beat the cadence for military men in the area—including George Washington, for a few days.

Now Chatham is a place to pass through on the way to someplace else, just as it was in the beginning. Its 8,000 or so residents calmly (more or less) watch the ebb and flow of traffic, even as they identify with their historic structures, step out for celebratory bands, and cheer for the home teams.

Today's Chathamites are cosmopolitan and urbane. They know who they are, where their history has taken their ancestors and themselves, and what transpires in town day-by-day. Nearly all of them are pleased to be here.

John T. Cunningham
Spring 1997

One
River of Dreams

Little boys always have known the Passaic River as a place to relive the epic of Huck Finn, to fish, skip stones on the surface, row boats, and swim (before bacterial counts). Adults used the river to run mills. Romantic visitors saw it as a spot for memorable interludes.

Seen from the stone railroad bridge near Stanley on the southern end of town in less frenetic days, the slowly moving Passaic River in its normal springtime mood was serene, as this magnificent portrait snapped by an unknown photographer demonstrates.

Vividly in contrast with the stream on the opposite page, this is the Passaic in an angry, violent spring mood, caught by a *Newark Evening News* photographer in March 1934. A severe winter, followed by spring rains, raised the river level and tossed huge ice floes across the landscape.

The Stanley dam and raceway, the most southerly dam within Chatham limits, typified dreams of bucolic childhoods when this photograph was taken in 1870. Tradition says that a noted nineteenth-century character named "Black Betsy" lived in the large, prominent frame house.

Printed on a postcard early in the twentieth century, this was a nostalgic scene for the many summer visitors who loved the wide waterfall over a Passaic River Dam. Many people sent home cards with the time-honored "wish you were here" message.

It wasn't exactly the crest of Niagara Falls, but early-twentieth-century rowers found at least mild excitement when they ventured close to the top of the Parrot Mill Dam. In spring, high flood waters made capsizing a distinct possibility. Several children drowned here.

Winter embellishes the appearance of Day's Brook as it meanders under the Weston Avenue walkway toward its rendezvous with the Passaic River. This small stream is the only Chatham geographical landmark that still bears the name of the town's founding family.

The males atop the dam were not mere spectators watching friends dive into swirling waters beneath the dam (probably Edwards). Rather, they protected their skinny-dipping buddies in case potentially easily embarrassed people (such as girls) wandered nearby.

Destined to be the most picturesque span ever to carry travelers over the river in Chatham, the so-called high bridge was anything but beautiful as it neared completion in 1874. This photograph was taken by the erector, the Phillipsburg Manufacturing Company.

Within twenty years after the scene above was captured, the "high bridge" had the kind of classical appearance that adorns the jackets of English adventure novels. For all the tree-shaded beauty, the span faced demolition as the 1890s wore on. It had sagged nearly 7 inches in a quarter century.

Quaintness was out when the then-newest Main Street bridge was completed in 1909. Cement was in vogue for highway roadbeds and bridges. During construction, builders and archaeologists uncovered five ancient roadbeds, probably including John's Day's low-level span.

Concrete bridges, with some aging and proliferation of trees, took on their own dignity. So it was with the Main Street bridge, gracefully arched in the manner of park bridges of the time. This bridge provided the "tickle bump" familiar to several generations of Chatham children.

Two
Establishing a Town

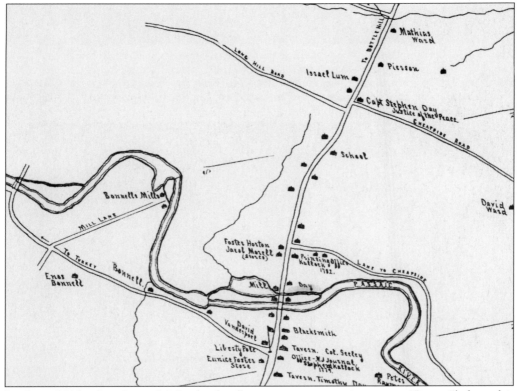

In about 1915, when James M. Littlejohn (known to everyone in town as "Jimmy") drew this Revolutionary War map, his research showed a town on both sides of the Passaic River, with most business establishments east of the stream. At least three dams were in place, powering mills. Only four streets went outward from the principal thoroughfare, which was then unnamed. Important families in local history—Bonnell, Day, and Lum—were well established on Littlejohn's map.

The "Three Towns Pageant," conceived and carried out by residents of Madison, Chatham, and Summit, made history seem alive in such scenes as the arrival of settlers on the banks of the Fishawack River. Even if the horses looked like those from the Budd farm and the Conestoga wagon was about fifty years before its inclusion in American history, the pageant still crystallized historical enthusiasm in the area.

Excitement at the pageant neared a peak when these settlers clustered outside of "John Day's Tavern" (a replica, 1926-style). Nearly 13,000 spectators, the largest crowd ever seen in the area, clustered around the meadow that served as an open-air stage. The *Newark Evening News* said the pageant "exceeded in magnitude and detail" anything in the region's history.

A "Lenape Indian" family pleased the crowd, although purists knew that such costumes, footwear, and head adornments were never worn by Lenapes. The male in the center is Merritt Lum Budd, who later became a top Native American authority. To the left is his wife, Edna VanSickle Budd, and their son, Merritt Lum Jr. To the right is Kate Hallet.

Lined up beside the Fishawack in full view of 13,000 or so people, the Chatham Lenapes (they called themselves the Minisinks) had an air of majesty, although they were about to lose their

land to settlers who had come out of the sun (from the east) to push them aside. The costumes
tended to be fanciful but the spirit was infectious.

One of the oldest houses still standing on Chatham's Main Street, this dwelling was built in late 1780 or early 1781 by William Day, soon after he and Nancy Bonnell were married. The wedding united two of Chatham's most important early families. This photograph was taken about 1910.

The well-preserved Daniel Bower House on Hillside Avenue was moved from its original location on Fairmount Avenue. Ben Lyons, railroad employee, who lived in the house at the end of the nineteenth century, added the front porch. Lyons talked to his wife only "through" their cat.

The village by John Day's bridge finally chose a lasting name in 1773, paying tribute to William Pitt, The Elder, first Earl of Chatham in England. Pitt sympathized with America's quest for liberty and vigorously opposed King George III's tax policies aimed at colonists. The Earl of Chatham's seal is in the lower right corner.

Built in 1740, the Jacob Morrell House at 63 Main Street, Chatham's most significant early building, has survived termites, frequent neglect, and many alterations. General George Washington is believed to have stayed in the house for two or three days in late August 1781 while he marshaled his forces for the march to Yorktown, Virginia.

This is a sketch of Shepard Kollock, who wrote and printed the *New-Jersey Journal* in Chatham. The paper was established in February 1779 to spread Continental Army propaganda. Popularly called "The Chatham Paper," the *Journal* had little local news in its government-controlled pages.

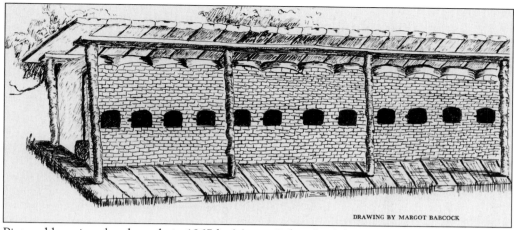

DRAWING BY MARGOT BABCOCK

Pictured here is a sketch made in 1967 by Margot Babcock of the Chatham bake ovens, based on early accounts. When Washington assembled troops in Chatham in August 1781 for the advance to Yorktown, he ordered brick ovens built, large enough to feed 5,000 soldiers, in an attempt to delude the British into thinking he planned to attack New York. The hoax was a complete success.

Pictured here is Charles Asgill, a nineteen-year-old British captain who was imprisoned in Chatham from June to November 1781. He awaited hanging in revenge for the British execution of an innocent Monmouth County captain. The Continental Congress, after fierce debate, agreed to free Asgill.

New Jersey's first toll road, the Morris Turnpike, was finished through town in 1804. Pikes, or toll booths, such as this one just east of Chatham bridge, took in the shillings to maintain the 34-foot-wide road. Those seeking to avoid tolls took the "shunpike" south of town.

Anticipating the turnpike, William Day built this tavern near the bridge. It served travelers and drovers who herded pigs and sheep to city markets. This photograph shows the building in the early twentieth century. The place was destroyed in 1965 by a fire, likely set by an arsonist.

Originally built in 1806 on Main Street near the center of town, this is the famed Chatham Academy, the second school in the village. It was moved from Main Street to Summit Avenue in 1873 to make space for the Presbyterian chapel. The old school is now a two-family residence.

MAIN STREET, CHATHAM, 1845

Ubiquitous historians John W. Barber and Henry Howe visited Chatham in about 1842. Their resulting woodcut showed Main Street eastward from Summit Avenue to the river. The Methodist church is in the right foreground, and the Presbyterian steeple is to the distant left.

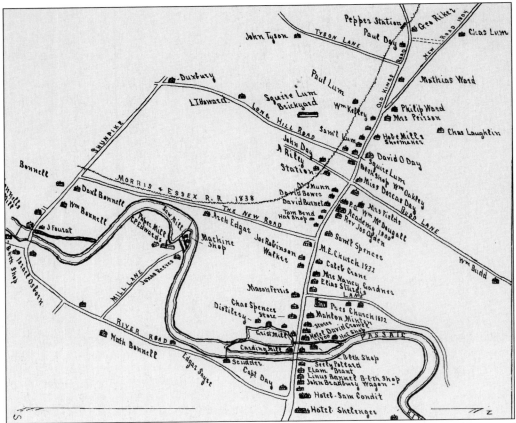

Jimmy Littlejohn, in a map drawn shortly before World War I, depicted Chatham at the time of the Barber and Howe visit. (Jimmy labeled Summit Avenue "The New Road.") Budd Lane (now Passaic Avenue) had been cut through. Most lots on Main Street, on both sides of the river, were occupied.

Bonnell's Dam in the southeast section of town had long been in place by the time of Littlejohn's map. Note the cluster of Bonnells along the Shunpike in the map above. Note, too, that the Morris & Essex Railroad had entered town, curving sharply westward, away from the river.

Pictured here is the William Bonnell homestead at the corner of Watchung Avenue (Shunpike) and River Road in about 1890. By then it was occupied by James T. Wagner, a member of the Chatham Borough Council representing the "Stanley Section."

Hudson Minton's general store and post office on the corner of Long Hill Road (now Fairmount Avenue) and Main Street was a town social center when this scene was snapped in about 1890. Note the boy on the wooden bicycle. Erected in about 1850, the store was eventually replaced by a bank.

Three

The Way to Go

Chatham's unofficial "greeters" of nearly every train in the late 1890s were, from left to right, as follows: Mike Roach, railroad track walker; George Dennis, baggage master; Hank Ryerson, daily depot visitor; and Charles Riker, keeper of the Passaic Avenue gates.

Chatham's railroad station is presented here in a posed photograph, taken in 1876 or 1877. The platform crowd included engineer Ed Taylor, several local merchants, and the usual track-side

onlookers. Ben Baldwin, one of the town's few black residents, is at the baggage truck on the right. The depot style was typical on this railroad.

Perched on the railroad tracks atop the sturdy stone span that carried the railroad across the Passaic River in about 1900, a man and his dog had the best bird's-eye view in town. The impressive span, an enduring town landmark, is about 400 feet east of Stanley Park.

Although this was only a few blocks from Chatham center in the 1890s, this portion of South Passaic Avenue looked like a tree-shaded country village. The "Stop, Look & Listen" sign and the long white gates warned of grade-level railroad tracks. The view is looking toward Main Street.

The depot is pictured here in about 1910, before the tracks were elevated through town. The time of day was likely mid-afternoon, perhaps in summer, when out-of-town vacationers could be expected to arrive. The horse-drawn carriages would be hacks waiting to take such visitors to town hotels.

George Dennis (left) and Charlie Riker were certain day-to-day visitors at the depot. Could there have been a more stress-free life than lounging in the sun and discussing and solving the problems of the world—if they were not too distant from Chatham's sheltered life?

Adolescent boys found heroes aboard the "drill," an unpretentious little engine that switched cars in the yard, boosted heavy freight trains up the hill to Summit, and offered a chance to ride on the front bumpers on return trips from Summit.

Can you imagine being a child in about 1910 when the circus train stopped for water and fuel, allowing a performer and his bear to alight? The visitors put on their act, of course, anticipating a few pennies. In the distance beyond the bear's head can be seen Chatham's large roundhouse.

Rounding the long curve leading into Chatham's railroad yard, a train steams westward from Summit. The painter's car on the siding in the foreground is not for a group of wandering artists but served as the workaday quarters of a crew sprucing up the depot and other buildings.

Long lineups of horses and heavy wagons streamed through the freight yard on Bowers Lane in about 1900. The railroad was Chatham's economic lifeline, bringing in coal, dry goods, bolts of cloth, food, and nearly everything else needed. It took out products from mills and greenhouses.

Excitement swirled about the little Postal Telegraph office on Watchung Avenue. Telegraph wires brought messages and startling news, plus notices of births, deaths, and marriages, or messages from visitors. It wasn't all work at the office, however. The hammock in front wasn't just for local color.

William McDougall, peripatetic local photographer, posed telegraph linemen as they were stringing new wires into Chatham in the 1890s. The wires were apparently fastened to three cross arms at ground level, and then arms and wires were lifted into place and attached to poles.

Railroad men were local heroes. Such a man was Edward Taylor, engineer on the local train known as the Chatham Accommodation. Taylor was a member of the first Borough Council elected in 1898.

Chatham teemed with action when the Delaware, Lackawanna & Western Railroad elevated its roadbed through town just before World War I. This was one of the new bridges under construction, looking southeast along Watchung Avenue. The house on the left is still standing.

People on Lafayette Avenue had cause to wonder whether the elevated railroad bridge across their street would ever be finished. In a time of steam-powered equipment and manual work achieved mainly by men and mules, a project of this magnitude took many months to finish.

This remarkable photograph shows, among other things, both the new, elevated station and the old ground-level depot a block to the east (right foreground). By 1916, the telephone poles would be removed, the tracks laid, and the new station opened. Remarkably, the trains never stopped running.

In 1916 the elevation crews cleared away the debris, loaded their machines aboard flatcars, and left town. Powerful steam locomotives pulled trains across the Passaic River bridge and headed westward from Summit toward Chatham, Madison, the Pocono mountains, and Buffalo, New York.

Real Estate Office of Edna Dickinson
Chatham, N.J.

Edna Dickinson's real estate office near the new station often appeared on postcards. The Greek Revival-style building later became the police station and remained so until 1985, when all municipal offices were consolidated in the old Fairmount Avenue School on the other side of the tracks.

Northeast of the station was Reasoner Park, once an unsightly railroad property, which became a park in 1896. The railroad donated the property and supplied fill dirt. Townspeople laid out a park and planted grass. The town named the park for railroad superintendent Andrew Reasoner.

It will never be known whether Mr. and Mrs. Clarence Hand and their children were coming or going on the railroad. For that matter, they might merely have been walking through Reasoner Park after attending church services. Such park tours were a favored Sunday afternoon diversion.

"Commuters" and "Chatham" became virtual synonyms after the Civil War. Nearly a century had elapsed after the Civil War when this crowd was snapped leaving a commuter train in town. Hundreds of thousands of feet have climbed and descended these elevated stairs since 1916.

Wood-burning locomotives spewed sparks over passengers when Addison Day began commuting from Chatham to New York City in 1869. He entered the city 20,000 times, rode more than one million miles in commuting cars, and was a local hero on this last trip on June 21, 1934.

The first trolley came to Chatham in February 1912, after overcoming severe opposition in town. The new form of transportation was quickly accepted, and was soon valued as a comfortable, dependable way to reach neighboring towns and Newark's fine shops, movies, and restaurants.

Trolleys ran east and west every half hour. They took about thirty minutes longer than a train from Chatham to Newark, but they were cheaper and in summertime considerably more comfortable. The trolleys spurred railroads into vastly improved and more courteous service.

Trolley car conductors were never quite the heroes that railroad men were, and they were rarely singled out for photographs. In this picture is notable Chatham car conductor Raymond Whiteman, who left his livery service at the Fairview House to collect 5¢ streetcar fares.

Railroaders and trolley fans laughed at the thought that the first automobiles were competition. Too many drivers were stranded when they wandered away from roads in established settlements. Abner Reeves, a local garage owner, suffered this fate while on a trip in Sussex County.

Chatham officials knew how to take care of upstart motorists. They passed a law limiting top speeds through town to 10 miles per hour. The signs tacked on trees said the ordinance "prohibits greater speed." It is not known how many defied the statute.

This was a bit in fun, but only a bit. The chauffeur of the wealthy Vanderpoel family car was being ribbed by the Vanderpoel's ever-vigilant private policeman. However, the guard would have arrested the chauffeur or anyone else encroaching on the Vanderpoel's property.

One of the first automobiles in Chatham meanders east past Dr. Wolfe's Pharmacy, at the corner of Main and Passaic. The double trolley tracks tended to narrow the street for automobiles. The tracks also were extremely dangerous in rainy or snowy weather.

Dr. William J. Wolfe, who owned the huge building at the corner of Main Street and Passaic Avenue, proudly showed off his electric-powered Milburn car in about 1920. The vehicle featured solid rubber tires, space for batteries, and a single door centered in the body.

People in Chatham (and their visitors) finally knew where they were—as long as they related to the nine towns on this directional billboard erected in about 1920. Polarine, befitting the automobile age, was a motor lubrication made by the Standard Oil Company.

Four
Old Main Street

The Day family had been looking out on Main Street for ninety-five years and five generations when daguerreotype makers from the Crystal Palace Exposition visited Chatham in 1853 to capture the five "Day girls." They are, from left to right, as follows: (front row) Mrs. Day, 93; her daughter, Mrs. Sally Crane, 77; and Mrs. Day's granddaughter, Mrs. Nancy Gardner, 49; (back row) Mrs. Gardner's daughter, Mrs. Sarah Crane, 32; and Sarah's daughter, Joanna, 8. The adult ladies wore black silk, while Sarah sported a bright frock.

Striding down Main Street in about 1895, Mace Ferris was a strong, confident neighbor to cameraman George McDougall, who took many of the older photographs in this volume. The curious little boy in the left background may have been Willie McDougall, son of George.

By 1910 the Day family, whose fortunes and community ties began at the Passaic River on the eastern edge of town, had a large open property on west Main Street. One of the attractions was the much-used tennis court, where a game official controlled action from atop a stepladder.

Even light snow turned nineteenth-century Main Street dirt into mud. This scene is just west of Fairmount Avenue. The fencing on each side was erected early in the century to keep sheep and hogs from invading local yards as they were driven toward Newark and Elizabeth markets.

Fog pervaded Main Street when this surprise spring snowstorm hit, covering the early blossoms surrounding Nelson Kelley's white farmhouse (center). This appalled Mrs. Kelley, who was described by a contemporary as a "frail and sweet woman, tending each plant in her lovely garden."

Benjamin P. ("Squire") Lum built this carriage house behind the home of his son, Benjamin Jr., at 295 Main Street. The main house and this structure were built in about 1865. Noted New Jersey artist Harry Devlin painted a view of this historic Lum building.

Perhaps the most prominent building ever to adorn Main Street was the Wolfe Building, on the corner of South Passaic Avenue. The building, erected in 1897 by Dr. William J. Wolfe, provided him with a home, an office, rental stores, and a large meeting hall, which was used by many local groups.

Planning and preservation were not in vogue in 1928, when the Wolfe Building was demolished to make way for these useful stores. Later, the Patterson family wares (beer, wine, and newspapers) made this one of the borough's most-frequented corners.

Any major snowstorm brought a hush to Main Street in the slow-paced days before World War I. Minton's historically acclaimed store is on the right, at the corner of Fairmount and Main. The early electric lamp in the center of the street was a source of village pride.

The snow is gone, but the pace was not much faster. A buggy driver paused to talk with a neighbor. While waiting for the photographer (likely George McDougall) to click the shutter, the driver heard no horns. Beyond the buggy is Dr. George Swaim's office (now the Cafe Beethoven).

Crisp white dresses, a lawn setting, and a sense of dignity; such were requisites for ladies when Main Street residents Mrs. William Ogden and her two daughters, Anna (left) and Nana, posed for a visiting commercial photographer in 1905.

Main Street children grew up quietly, as did most children of the late nineteenth century. Here Alvin Mead, son of the proprietor of the hardware store at the corner of Center and Main Streets, poses with his dog Jimmy for Ivan McKee Smith in the yard at the rear of the store.

Willie McDougall, son of the photographer, was the most photographed kid in town. Here he spent the best part of an afternoon playing with his pet goat while his father waited for exactly the right sun exposure to coincide with good action.

56

Young Raymond Whiteman, who traveled by train to Morristown to have this image taken in a studio, grew up to be an owner of his own prosperous livery stable. He later became a conductor on the trolley line through town.

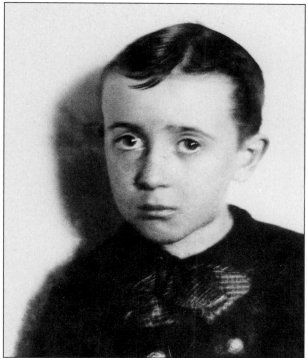

Here is an up-close look at Willie McDougall. He stared out at his dad and the world with big sad eyes, overwhelmed by the ever-present childhood awareness that some photographic sessions with one's father seem to last forever.

Straw hat tilted and the Sunday comics momentarily set aside, young George McDougall, whose photographs illuminate much of Chatham's late-nineteenth-century history, had the tables turned on him when someone else held the camera. The bright socks were sartorial splendor for the day.

The McDougall family gathered for a rare family portrait that included three generations, including Willie, of course. They posed in the parlor.

Mrs. William McDougall, George's mother, poses patiently on the front steps of the Main Street family home in a classic photograph of a family matriarch, her face creased by decades of tiring, often difficult, nineteenth-century life.

George McDougall, normally the dashing Main Street cameraman, strikes a relaxed pose in front of lush grapevines and flower beds. Note the folding wooden lawn chair and foot rest. Mrs. McDougall, his second wife, looks on adoringly. Her first name is not known.

Whenever the McDougalls (and many other Main Street residents) yearned for a bit of country scenery, all they had to do was look outward across their back yards. Family cows grazed serenely on pastures that stretched away almost as far as the eye could see.

The two Mrs. McDougalls are pictured here at ease. The photograph above is of the first Mrs. McDougall, with her son Willie (smiling at last) astride his popular little tricycle. The second Mrs. McDougall is in the photograph below, relaxing in the wooden easy chair that George occupies in the illustration on p. 58. The Fairview Annex is on the other side of the McDougall's yard.

The five generations of the Day, Smith, and Crane families, pictured on p. 49, occupied this house at 76 Main Street for nearly a century. The above photograph was taken in the 1890s during the Crane family occupancy. The third floor and the east wing had been added, the latter as office space for Dr. George Swaim. The handsome house still stands (below), although unfortunately now without the spacious front porch and the nineteenth-century picket fence. In the 1960s Ray Ellis, the nationally prominent watercolor artist, occupied the first floor.

South Passaic Avenue, formerly East Park Street, looking toward Main Street, included such shops as Scherer's bakery, a Chinese laundry, a wagon shop, and a grocery store. The old wooden buildings were removed in the 1960s when the Post Office Mall was built.

Pictured here is "Kelley's Elbow," developed in the 1880s by Frank Kelley, Main Street grocery store owner and second mayor of Chatham. The street (now Center Street) went north from Main, then turned ninety degrees to Passaic Avenue. The houses still stand, except the one nearest the camera.

One of the three much-admired "Victorians" built in the 1880s by Paul Lum, the Gothic Revival house above at 95 Fairmount Avenue was first occupied by Sarah Heald, a member of the Edwards family that operated mills along the Passaic River. Later, Raymond St. James Perrin, a Columbia University professor, lived here. In the twentieth century, the Spohrs (three brothers) and Groberts (four boys) occupied the house, one family after the other. In this period the place became the more modern house below.

Summit Avenue was laid out early as the road to neighboring Summit. In about 1910, when this photograph was taken, the railroad yards bustled with activity; and this street led to the huge roundhouse. The old Methodist parsonage is on the left; on the right is the Edward Harris House (since demolished). In contrast, the photograph below, looking south from Fairmount toward the Edgehill development, shows the Genung homestead, with Hudson Muchmore's house to the rear. An 1876 developer went bankrupt here, after building about six houses.

Tales of the much-vaunted "good old days," when snow supposedly was deeper, get credence from the snow on either side of Passaic Avenue, near the bridge, on February 12, 1895.

OPPOSITE: Frank L. Moore shovels his walk on Fairmount Avenue in around 1888.

Chatham Borough's first mayor, Frederic K. Lum, could view Main Street and the rest of newly created Chatham Borough with satisfaction after his election in 1897. By then the Lums were the most prolific and prominent family in town. Frederic studied law in the Newark firm of Whitehead and Guild. He was admitted to the bar in 1870 and was accepted as a member of the firm. His heart and home were forever in Chatham but he won his fame and fortune in Newark.

Five

Feeding the Economy

Chathamites looked first to the river for economic sustenance, aware that damming the stream created tremendous waterpower. By 1845, four mills—and one distillery—were powered by the stream. The railroad created other jobs, from working on the railroad to commuting to work in the cities. This is the Edwards Dam as it looked in about 1890.

George Shepard Page, who had made a fortune by manufacturing crude tar and ammonia, came to Chatham in 1867 at age twenty-nine. He bought the Bonnell mills in the southeast portion

of town and converted them into a felt roofing-paper factory. The neat buildings blended well with the surrounding pasture land. Note the well-maintained split-rail fence in the foreground.

An unknown photographer climbed a high hill to get the above bird's-eye view of the Edwards Dam in winter. The Summit Avenue bridge can be seen in the distance. One of the major users of impounded water at the Edwards Dam was the Edwards Paper Company mill (below). The widespread cover on the water surface was caused by what one historian called water hyacinth, a plant that thrived on polluted waste from the manufacture of paper.

Summer visitors were big business, particularly at the Fairview House on Main Street (on the site now occupied by the Library of the Chathams). Dozens of local people worked at the hotel—clerks, bellboys, laundresses, maids, yardmen, cooks, waiters, painters, handymen, liverymen, and others. At its height, the hotel accommodated more than 150 guests, who came to enjoy the river and the nine-hole golf course. The Fairview also provided dancing, bowling, distinguished cuisine, and a large bar. Carriages entered the grounds through the Main Street arch (below).

Entrance to Fairview House, Chatham, N. J.

The occasion for this gathering at Snook's boarding house in about 1914 is not known, but since more than half of the young women were local school teachers who stayed at "The Snookery," it can be assumed it was in their honor. Jacob Snook, proprietor, also entertained summer visitors.

William A. Martin, a New York tea importer and wine merchant, built this Victorian mansion atop Fairmount Hill in the late 1850s. The upper right photograph was found during research for this book. Martin entertained lavishly, serving wine because it was "less costly than water."

Raymond Whiteman (the boy on p. 57) ran Whiteman's Livery stable (above), located on Passaic Avenue close to the Fairview House. His customers included Mrs. George Vanderpoel, who lived in the "castle" near the river. She always left a one dollar tip on the seat after a ride. A rival of Whiteman's was Dan Brown (below), whose hack met visitors at the station. This photograph was taken when Nellie VanOrden and her father arrived from Brooklyn for a summer vacation. The VanOrdens stayed in town, Nellie married a member of the Day family, and her son, Chon Day, became a nationally known cartoonist.

Main Street's business block in about 1900 contained stores that supplied almost everything—proprietary drugs, groceries, hardware, clothing, sweets, or whatever was needed or

Valentine & Mead's Hardware Store, corner of Main and Center, is shown here when kerosene street lamps were still in vogue. The wooden exterior was bricked over before 1920, but hardware was the lasting business until 1996, when wallpapers and fabrics replaced Swanson's Hardware.

desired. The owners and the nature of their businesses have changed, but at least the roof lines remain unchanged.

William McDougall's store and home was on Main Street, east of where the Library of the Chathams now stands. Son George, the photographer, later ran the store. In front is the ubiquitous and much-photographed Willie. The store, built in 1837, was demolished in 1947.

Soon after the Civil War, Nelson Kelley built this grocery store on the Kelley farmstead at the corner of Budd's Lane (now Passaic Avenue) and Main Street. His son Frank (developer of Kelley's Elbow) later ran the business. The upper floor was a town meeting room and social center, and in about 1875 the town library was opened here.

Reuben Marsh, called the "happy whistling man," stood beside Kelley's grocery wagon in about 1910. Marsh took orders in the morning and delivered the merchandise in the afternoon. It was a time when deliverymen also left bread and milk on front porches before dawn.

Four butchers await customers at Hatton's Market on South Passaic Avenue, just off Main Street. Customers were encouraged to sit on stools while choosing meats. They also could enjoy constantly hot coffee from the pot atop the barrel in the foreground.

Robinson's Pharmacy at Main and South Passaic occupied the ground floor of a residence, as did most businesses in town. Pharmacies were known as places for refreshment as well as medicine. Storefront signs advertised Horton's Ice Cream.

Except for fruit, loose cookies, and a few other items that customers could choose for themselves, merchandise in the Mutual Grocery Company store at the corner of North Passaic and Main was piled high on shelves behind the counter. One customer wore her roller skates into the store.

Frank Moore's Sunnywood greenhouses are pictured here in the 1920s. Rose growing was a vital industry; eleven growers had seventy separate greenhouses at the peak of Chatham's rose production. Competition from distant states eventually pushed the industry into eclipse. Sunnywood is now a section of homes on Fuller Circle.

James L. Littlejohn Sr. poses in front of his range (greenhouses) on Lum Avenue. He had seven of the "rose houses," one of the best spreads in town. The average greenhouse measured about 25 feet wide and 100 feet long.

Jimmy Littlejohn Jr. built his five greenhouses close to the railroad track, the better to secure coal brought in from Pennsylvania mines. Littlejohn gained substantial local fame by keeping a unique day-by-day diary for fifty-seven years, from 1887 until the day he died in 1943.

Edward P. Miller's coal pockets supplied many customers in town, including the large greenhouse owners. The coal storage was on Fairmount Avenue, close to the railroad tracks that brought in the fuel. The area is now part of the railroad's south-side parking lot.

Anthony Ruzicka bought the seven greenhouses of Samuel Lum in the western edge of town, modernized the complex, and vigorously marketed roses. The tall stack (top) was a constant reminder of his "Acres of Roses." Young people (below), mostly teen-aged boys, frolicked in the large pond that Ruzicka maintained to water his plants. The stack, the greenhouses, and the pond disappeared under the construction of the high school (now the Chatham Middle School).

George Page had sufficient capital when he came to Chatham to buy several hundred acres of land in the southeast edge of town. He refurbished several mills, persuaded the railroad to stop at Stanley (to honor his mother's family name), owned this store, and was Stanley's postmaster—and probably the wealthiest rural postmaster in the nation.

Six
Mind and Soul

Pictured here are Dr. Joseph M. Ogden (left), pastor of the Village Church of Chatham, and Helen Budd Gibby (right), the first person to leave town for higher education. Dr. Ogden served from 1828 to 1873, and was a spiritual and educational leader. Miss Budd left Chatham in 1855 to attend the just-founded Trenton Normal School, returned, taught school, married, and lived to be ninety-one.

The Village Church of Chatham (left), built in 1832 for a mere $3,132 (plus volunteer work), served as such until 1904, when the Ogden Memorial Presbyterian Church was erected. A portion of the old church building is now a real estate office. The handsome little Presbyterian chapel (below) became the home of St. Paul's Episcopal Church in 1904 as an exchange for the Episcopal-owned site, where the Ogden Memorial Church was built.

St. Paul's Episcopal Church, Chatham, N. J.   2178

Pictured here are the Methodist church and parsonage on Center Street. The church was built after a series of fund-raisers that included an oyster supper that "realized a good sum" at Kelley's Hall. It was dedicated in March 1899. Both church and parsonage have since been razed.

The first permanent St. Patrick's Church was this small brick building at Oliver and Washington Streets. It is now part of St. Patrick's School, having been replaced by the 820-seat church that was built and consecrated in 1955.

George Shepard Page, who started the Hillside Mission Sabbath School in 1867 in an outdoor setting, later built the stark two-story worship center (above), shown during construction. The pursuit of religion did not faze congregation rooftop daredevils when this photograph was taken in 1876. Walls of the first mission's small chapel (below) were papered with slogans paving the road to Heaven, although with dim lighting and poor ventilation the chapel was no Garden of Eden.

The Hillside Mission on the south side of town pondered a new "church on the hill," resulting in the founding of the Congregational Church, whose members built this first church in October 1884 at Hillside and Watchung Avenues. The building is now a handsome residence.

The decoration committee for the Christmas season in 1921 pleased worshippers at the Ogden Memorial Presbyterian Church with a colorful setting that, in addition to focusing on "Peace on Earth" and "Goodwill to Men," expressed the traditional sentiments of comfort and joy.

Neatly painted, with new windows in the old frames and dark shutters as adornment, the Hillside Mission also housed some school classes. The horse and buggy likely belonged to a visiting dignitary, as teachers were not affluent enough to own such equipage. The boys climbing trees perpetuated the adventurous spirit of their carefree older brothers (p. 88).

Boys and girls from all sections of Chatham entered Budd Lane School (above) in 1873. Constructed in the best Victorian fashion, the building featured a bell tower, separate entrances for boys and girls, and the newest of outdoor toilets. By the 1890s (below), getting to school was at least half the fun. Safety bicycles were in vogue. Of the six cycles, four were owned by girls. All of the boys wore caps; the two best-dressed women (likely teachers) fancied hats.

Patriotism had center stage at the Budd Lane School Washington Birthday observance in about 1900. Two boys in paper admiral-like hats led the class in singing about America and the Red, White, and Blue. Decorations included birds and blackboard song words that misspelled America as "Ameica."

Upper high school classes went to Summit until the new school opened in January 1911, in broad fields south of the railroad station. The building cost what many Chathamites felt was an exorbitant $8,000, but Chatham at last had a full K-12 program.

The first graduating class at the new Chatham High School received diplomas in 1911. In the above photograph the 1912 class, consisting of five girls and three boys, poses in front of the year-old school. The photograph below includes Charles A. Philhower (back row in suit), who was only two years out of college when he coached the 1911 Chatham High School football team. He also was superintendent of Chatham schools, a budding historian, and in time would become a noted New Jersey authority on Native American history.

Preston Lum, a member of one of Chatham's most distinguished (and largest) families, showed what a member of the 1912 high school eleven wore. A leather helmet protected his skull and his feet were well shod, but between head and ankles, his body had little protection.

Sporting the latest fashion, in full bloomers, shirts with rolled-up sleeves, scarves, black knee-high hose, and very high canvas sneakers, the 1921 Chatham High School girls basketball six (plus two substitutes) played a modest interscholastic schedule.

During the so-called Roaring Twenties, when the music of youth was vivid, the eleven-man Chatham High School jazz band was a popular fixture at high school and club parties. For no particular reason except that it was the style, the two drummers wore fashionable knickers.

Lynda Phillips Lum (left) refused to live the staid life of a lady. She studied library service, classified the 2,000 volumes in the old collection, and in 1907 became the borough's first librarian. After a World War I stint as a Coast Guard librarian, she led the way to the present library building, which opened on Main Street in 1924. The entire library interior is shown below. Soon after the library was opened, Miss Phillips married Dr. Frederick H. Lum Jr., and resigned from library service.

Seven
War and Peace

On the Fourth of July, 1917, with the first war against Germany only three months old, the annual parade honored those armed services involved in the American Revolution, the Civil War, the Spanish-American War, and World War I (the Red Cross, U.S. Navy, and U.S. Army). The symbol for peace stands in the center.

The Civil War and Union Army service lured Chatham's young men to distant fields. Thomas Phipps (top left) died of disease in Virginia on January 31, 1863. Several other local men never returned. Five Pollard brothers from Summit Avenue joined the cause. Eugene Pollard (bottom left) was imprisoned in the infamous Libby Prison in Richmond and later was badly wounded. Brother Will Pollard (bottom right) went to war at age eighteen.

Returning soldiers threw themselves into village life when the Civil War ended. Nothing in Chatham surpassed the cycling craze; to be a member of the Wheelmen's Club (above) insured acceptance in town. Smaller groups (below) often took varied trips on their own, riding into the country on their assorted wheels, old and new.

At the turn of the century, membership in the C.V.F.D. (Chatham Volunteer Fire Department) bestowed significant status on borough men. Note the horse-drawn hook and ladder truck in the rear (above.) By July 4, 1917, the department was motorized (below). Fred Walters, owner of a local lumberyard, is believed to be the man at the wheel.

The Chatham-organized Company B became part of the First Division when the United States entered World War I. Attired in campaign hats and laced-up puttees, the "boys" stood inspection during drilling at the school field. When the regulars went away, the town was protected by the Home Guard (below), marching snappily in the parade on July 4, 1917.

Frederick P. Parcells

Fred R. Pihlman

Paul Van Fleet

Eugene P. Hubbard

All five of Chatham's men who died in World War I were killed in France. Hubbard, first to die, was followed by Wolfe, Van Fleet, Parcells and Pihlman.

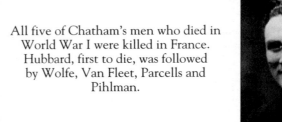

Van Horn D. Wolfe

Helen Johnson Miller (left) of Elmwood Avenue went to war as a "farmerette" (a female farm laborer), a partial solution to the acute labor shortages on Chatham area fields. Louise Page (right) became a volunteer Army nurse in 1917. Her husband was Harry Deb. Page, scion of a wealthy local family.

Chatham children in the 1930s and 1940s loved the bump sensation when the family car crossed the Main Street bridge. Eastward from the span was the Castle, with an atmosphere somewhere between spooky and romantic. It was the home of the very eccentric, and very rich, Vanderpoel family. Technically the home was across the river in Summit, but the family considered itself Chatham citizens. Ambrose Vanderpoel, son of the castle builder, wrote the *History of Chatham* in 1921.

George and Maria Ely Vanderpoel hired Harvey Lum of Chatham to build them a fourteen-room summer home in 1874. The house was destroyed on New Year's Eve in 1882, and the Vanderpoels built the second house (above), which is shown before it was altered, bricked over, and made into a castle. George Vanderpoel posed at the castle gate (below) with some of his prized cattle.

Mrs. Vanderpoel and her beloved son
Ambrose, who was born in the first summer
home in 1877, are pictured here. Ambrose
was described in his youth as "a cunning
little fellow." When he went to study at
Harvard, Mrs. Vanderpoel went along to
live in Cambridge, presumably to shield
the naive young man. Ambrose died a
recluse in 1940.

Maria Vanderpoel undoubtedly loved the summer home close to the Passaic River. She stayed there for long periods and at times walked near the dams in the river (above). She likely supervised the decoration of the music room (possibly the living room) in the castle, shown below as a relatively bare room in contrast to the Victorian penchant for over-decorating.

In 1940, with Europe embroiled in war, photographer Richmond Ross found serenity along Chatham's Main Street. His view was eastward toward the much-publicized and much-favored William Pitt Inn and Shop.

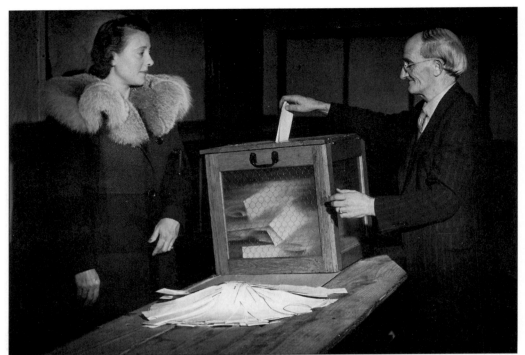

A smartly attired matron (above) cast her vote in the 1940 election for President of the United States. There were no mechanized voting booths; the old wooden and glass container had been recording local votes for decades. The annual Christmas party at the Fish and Game Club for Wealthy Ann Townsend's dancing class (below) was as traditional as Santa Claus. It was also traditional to stand and listen passionately when a swing band got into the groove.

Officer Ray Brink, long remembered for his proficiency as a policeman and his kindness to his constituents, guides two of Chatham's young misses across Watchung Avenue in 1940. Brink joined the department in 1937, became chief in 1947, and served in that capacity for seventeen years. No Chatham chief has ever served as long as Brink in the department's top job.

These pictures really need no caption; they tell the story of a moment of trust in 1941 when Dr. George Pike lightly touched a needle to the arm of a beaming young patient . . .

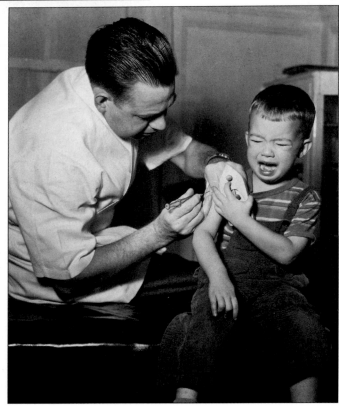

. . . and that moment of amazement after the needle had stung his flesh.

This high-school boy made the news in 1941—not by sawing wood but because shortly after this photograph was taken he cut off the tip of one finger in the Chatham High School woodworking shop.

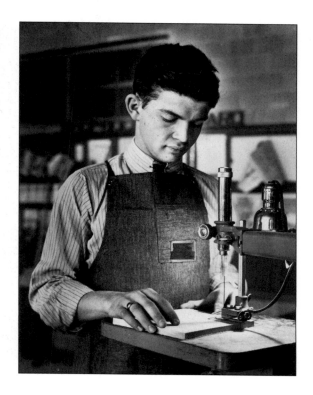

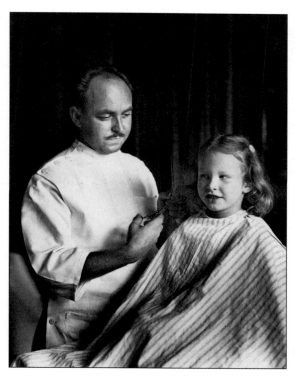

Here is another moment of truth, 1941 style: a Chatham barber is about to separate a young customer from her tresses. There is no room for error.

Alanson Bell

Edmund L. Berg

Charles W. Edgar

William B. Foster

Mortimer C. Huntsberger

Robert Hincham

Horace W. Johns

Nelson Kelley Jr.

Robert W. Kelley

All the sweet memories had to be put on hold when World War II took Chatham men around the world as part of the great force mobilized to whip the Axis Powers. The twenty-one Chatham men pictured on these two pages lost their lives—in France, Germany, Guadalcanal, the Philippines, Okinawa, and elsewhere. They died in many ways—by bullets, in accidents, plane crashes, ship sinkings, and aircraft fire. The world had shrunk in the shedding of blood of those who died on distant fields.

Charles L. Konecke

Arthur F. Messner Jr.

James A. Mousley Jr.

Robert D. Murphy

Raymond T. Napier

William A. Pieper

William W. Roberts

Peter C. Triolo

Burton M. Ward

Frank A. Wendell Jr.

John B. Wescott Jr.

Richard G. Wylie

For the first time, women joined men in the armed services. Representative of women who went to war was Helen McCabe, Seaman Second Class in the Coast Guard.

Civilians collected many things for the war effort—paper, tin, aluminum, iron, bottles, and other necessities once thrown away. Local Boy Scouts and Tony Carlone, who loaned his truck, took collected newspapers to a Delaware, Lackawanna & Western freight car for a quick trip to a recycling plant. Chatham (and many other communities) backed the civilian efforts with great zeal.

Eight

Only Yesterday

Although the conclusion of its first half-century of governing arrived in 1947, the Borough Council waited a year to celebrate, using a horse-drawn carriage in 1948's annual Fourth of July parade. In the background, Whalen & Berry's 5¢ to $1 store flourished. Its closing in the 1960s created a major void in Chatham.

Chatham is a celebrating town. Floats, such as this from a parade in the late 1930s, often featured the town's loveliest young women. Fourth of July parades usually have a patriotic motif or, in times of war, a strong show of support for the nation and its armed forces.

Except for variations in the clothing of both adults and children, the photograph on the right of the rapt attention exhibited by parade watchers could have been snapped almost any year. It actually was taken in 1940. That year residents watched such parade entries as an old time wagon drawn by matched oxen (above). Lady watchers on the curb felt that wearing a hat was de rigeur, even for a parade.

Can the Woman's Club of Chatham really date back to 1917 or, as some say, back to 1891 when its predecessor, the Ladies Reading Club, was founded? For that matter, is it possible that the still-popular swimming pool (below) off Passaic Avenue has been a source of joy for thousands of Chatham children since the 1920s, when it was built by the American Legion?

Modern celebrations include such things as long-distance runs, decorated T-shirts, and painted faces. These photographs by Jenny Fischer were taken on one of the Fishawack Days held every other year to honor (more or less) the name given the Passaic River by the Lenape Indians. The river name became popular soon after publication in 1967 of the Chatham Historical Society's history, *Chatham: At the Crossing of the Fishawack*, a notable community-wide effort.

Brooklyn-born Richard Gerdau, who grew up in the borough from age six and graduated from Chatham High School in 1964, gave Chatham an hour of national attention in the 1977 ABC television documentary, *The Class That Went to War.* It focused on Chatham High School's class of 1964 to portray the dilemma facing young people during the Vietnam War and to show the often shoddy treatment accorded returning veterans.

Chatham casualties in that war, as they appear on the town Vietnam War plaque, were Stephen J. Hadley, Guy F. Johnson, Robert B. Gilray Jr., and Manuel L. Font.

120

Three of the leaders who helped Chathamites express themselves for more than eighty-five years are shown here. Herbert Strong (left) wrote and staged *Amanda Minton's Dream* in 1912 to underwrite the purchase of seats for the high school auditorium. He also helped put on the huge pageant of 1926. Major Herbert M. Dawley (center) was a movie-maker, sculptor, and prime mover in founding the Chatham Community Players in 1921. Edouard Martin (right), known as "Toot" Martin, became a leading light in the Players after World II and wrote the company's history in 1996, shortly before he died.

The Community Players gained a permanent home in 1967 by acquiring Legion Hall on Passaic Avenue. Volunteers immediately began refurbishing the one-time hay and seed store. Originally built on Fairmount Avenue, the building was relocated when the railroad tracks were elevated.

CHATHAM COMMUNITY PLAYERS

The Community Players have entertained theatergoers for over seventy-five years with both serious plays and song-and-dance, as in the chorus line (above) from a production of the 1920s. After the 100th presentation (over several years) of *A Christmas Carol*, the various casts gathered to celebrate in 1994 (below).

This photograph of volunteer musical aides is titled "Semi-Conductors," understandable in an area where scientific research makes such titles doubly appropriate. The little baton wavers were behind the Chatham Community Band as it made music in the borough gazebo. This photograph and the one below were taken by Jenny Fischer.

Jared Moore, born in 1894, lived long enough to experience at least five wars (including World War I, where he served in uniform), the nation's worst depression, the election and re-election of fourteen U.S. Presidents, and a century of international turmoil. He died at age one hundred.

Federal and state delays made completion of Route 24 a mockery for more than thirty years, sending heavy traffic streaming up overloaded Main Street. Council candidate (later Mayor) Jacquelyn Marvin-Maucher and fellow candidate William Hayes campaigned to complete the long-stalled Route 24, and the state highway was finally opened in 1992 (see p. 127).

Founded in 1936 as part of the Chatham Volunteer Fire Department, the rescue squad became the independent Chatham Emergency Squad on July 1, 1951. Dick Richards (left), Bill Swenson (center), and Balcolm Parcells pose beside their immaculate stork-adorned ambulance in front of the squad home built in 1954.

The painting above has special significance: it displays both the talent of Chatham's nationally known artist Ray Ellis and his watercolor of the William Pitt Inn, which opened in 1933 and was destined to become one of New Jersey's finest eating places. The fabled inn caught fire one early February morning in 1985 and was destroyed, as shown in the photograph below by Joe Marts.

Eventually the D.L.&W.'s old (some said ancient; no one said beloved) green cars were replaced by modern commuting cars. The latest management, the New Jersey Department of Transportation, now even offers direct service into midtown New York City.

In the early 1920s, a tiny lunch wagon opened on Main Street and served until this Chatham Diner replaced it. Anthony Tunnero, proprietor, retired in 1990 after about forty years of preparing diner fare. Chinese and Mexican menus have been recent features.

Looking south in 1972, as builders of Route 24 were spreading concrete across the landscape, the Passaic River seemed beautiful and eternal. Eventually, when substantial commercial buildings rose on the Chatham side of the river to the right, the Passaic (well, Fishawack) became increasingly difficult to see. The experience of actually crossing a river on an identifiable span became the stuff of memory.

And so the borough came of age, if reaching one hundred years is coming of age. These surviving mayors celebrating the centennial in 1997 are, from left to right, as follows: Joseph L. Marts (1976–79), the only Democrat; Jacqueline Marvin-Maucher (1984–87), Chatham's first woman mayor; John H. Bennett (1980–83); and Barbara L. Hall, who took office in 1988 and was in office during the centennial year.